BODILY FLUIDS

Len Lukowski is a writer based in Glasgow. His pamphlet, *The Bare Thing* was published by Broken Sleep Books in 2022. This is his first full length collection.

Also by Len Lukowski

The Bare Thing   (Broken Sleep Books, 2022)

CONTENTS

ISBN: 978-1-917617-30-7

Cover designed by Aaron Kent

Edited and Typeset by Aaron Kent

Broken Sleep Books Ltd
PO BOX 102
Llandysul
SA44 9BG

Bodily Fluids

Len Lukowski

Broken Sleep Books

Happy are we when we choose to wear the blindfold
And mark our own place with the smell of our own

— The Hidden Cameras

OLYMPIAN

It's the nineties and I'm sitting on the sofa watching the Olympics
          with my dad.

Three muscular, supple men are standing on the podium, flags are
          waving,
dad is close to crying because his favourite won.

The man who got gold has his medal presented by his Olympic
          athlete girlfriend,
there are whispers he will propose. The girlfriend steps back to
          give him room.

As the crowd cheer the Gold holds his trophy up to the sky, turns
          and bends
slightly to kiss the man to his right who won the Silver, fully and
          with tongue.

The camera pans to the girlfriend's face which is white with horror.
The Bronze is joining in now, grabbing the arse of the Gold as he
          continues to kiss

the Silver, hands creeping down sweaty jockstraps. I spot you in
          the crowd
though I have yet to meet you. You take a lighter from your pocket

and set a flag on fire. The three men dismount from the podium
          and the Silver

bites the Gold's neck, lifting his vest, licking his smooth pec, down
            to the nipple.

More flags burn and in the flames I see our friendship played out
            over time.
I will live above a pub in the same small city as you, for years we'll
            never meet.

When we finally do, we'll go to Berlin together, to sex parties in
            cold squats,
too shy to get laid. The years will shift again, we'll both be middle
            aged,

cycling from Glasgow to Loch Lomond, my wheels squeaking like
            a mouse
splattered repeatedly. The nights between, some good, some

resulting in hard-edged shame. A group of us huddled on the beach
            in Brighton
under cold moonlight, passing a bottle of whiskey between us. You
            and me waltzing

beneath a shopping centre in Leeds to a gravelly-voiced woman
            singing
about wanting to die. The person in the Stadium who may or may
            not be

you drops the burning flag before the flames reach their fingers.
The whole auditorium is on fire now and the Gold is in a spit roast
            between the Silver

and the Bronze, who are thrusting as only Olympians can thrust,
        sweat glinting
on firm chests and I don't understand what's happening but I know
        I want the same.

Dad looks at the TV like the world is ending, but it's only beginning.

BODILY FLUIDS

I will say this categorically, you cannot change your sex. Your sex actually is there in every single cell of the body. You have a chromosomal sex, you have genetic sex, hormonal sex, psychological, brain sex, they are all different.
— Professor Robert Winston, *BBC Question Time*, 2021

Robert,

this morning

I was thinking

about what you said

as I was applying

the outsourced

part of myself —

the testosterone

suspended

in glistening

alcoholic gel

to my shoulders

and arms

and an errant

splodge

broke free

from my

fingertips and fell

upon a scrapbook

on the floor

into which

I'd just been

pasting a poem.

No place in nature we could meet — that one.

And Robert, it looked
like a globule of sweat, of cum,
just another bodily fluid.
There's a nature
that comes
from within us
and one
from outside
and sometimes
they're both
things at once
and sometimes
they swap places
and sometimes
it's impossible
to tell the difference
all our bodies
a museum
to the things
we've been
through. I'm not
going to argue
with you Robert
because you're a scientist
and I'm just here
but I used to be a librarian
and I know about categorical
systems of classification
how sometimes
they need updating.

This morning though
I watched
with curiosity
as the blob dried
in seconds
on the book's brown
cardboard cover
stripping away a layer
forever changing
its composition
a little universe
in the shape of a splatter.

FUGUE AFTER THE GYM

Burn
you're breathing
real air
not the shallow
intakes you're used to
alive to the city
the birds
the low thrum of doom
made by helicopters
all of it
this is the way
to stay sane
when therapy
costs too much and
the drugs wear off
and it's all crashing
inwards
to a place
where everything hurts
and nothing hurts.
Lay upon the shag Ikea
rug, soak it with sweat,
this is how you stay
with nothing
but the burn
and the surety
you kept things at bay
another 24 hours

muscles relaxing

demons tap

at the trap door

to your skull

pushed back

by the endorphinous wave

retreat but never

leave completely

this is how you stay

in one place

this is how you hold onto something

hold on

ODE TO VEGA

Oh claw-handed smooth-bodied dancing assassin
I want to run my fingers across your pixel muscles
and follow with my tongue
oh pretty boy
oh pony-tailed matador
half man half woman
you wake up the queer in me
take my clumsy
teenage flesh
that smells of insecurity
and lend me your grace
your colour your fight
right now resilience
is all I have
and there has to be more
than just
surviving to the end

trans angel that flies
and wears a mask
like all the fags at the ball
claw my 3D form
and draw blood.
You who can dance
and sing
at healing pitch
and fight with the
strength of a ballerina.

I knew you were queer

before I knew what queer was

and though I am not beautiful

or graceful

and cannot sing

or dance or fight

I knew I must be too.

Did my beauty intoxicate you?

Of course it did. K.O.

WHO AM I?
A cento of Bob's letters

I am for once not sauna-bound
I go to roller discos and play the violin
I feel very lucky and weirdly undeserving

I'd say a good third of my day is spent fobbing people off
Sometimes I feel like I'm just living out this tired, homosexual cliche
repeated on a loop, just with different music and different medication

I go on Instagram and look at the drag cycles of Kent
in my brown lederhosen
I don't think I convinced anyone that I was into leather

I'm listening to Tchaikovsky's violin concerto
which makes everything sound more dramatic than it actually is
It took me hours to hacksaw my way through a kitchen knife

I've got very good at disassociating
I guess this is what a lifetime of precarity does to the psyche
we shouldn't beat ourselves up

I don't think we could have moved further away from each other
One day I'll set up a sex club and it'll be like the set of Fun House
I'm slowly beginning to trust the sense of home

I MAKE PEOPLE INTO MY DAD

When I let some fucking asshole have me I just go with whatever
        he wants
I'm bad when I don't know what people want, I always make the
        wrong decision
I thought I was a total prick for not just giving you what you
        wanted
I'm telling you I can't be saved
I can say for sure I have a cute ass
I've jacked off thinking about you holding me in your arms
I don't want to talk about the details anymore

IN THE HEAT

of the fuck
in the heat of being used
and topped
you sell yourself short
forgetting who you are.

That's all your
YouPorn-fed
imagination
is capable of
sell yourself short
call out the things
from movies
the people with
the same anatomy say.

And it works -
to turn him on
to turn you on
are you really
surprised after
when he forgets
you're a guy?

The shame can only
be rubbed out
with a sharp exit
and buying something,

staring into a book
you're not reading
as coffee arrives
and you pour white milk in
longing to come
on somebody's
mouth, chest, heart.

OUTTAKES

A man is lying on his back in a bed, shot
from above we see only his head and neck

and the legs and hard on of the man
straddling his face and holding the camera

lick my balls, lick my balls
the cameraman is saying, *good boy*

the reclining man removes his mouth
from around the balls

bursts out laughing and
the top starts laughing too.

I'm not your good boy,
says the bottom,

you're my *good boy!*
The caption above

says something
about the downsides

of filming with your
best friend. I always

thought sex that was hot
could only be dark

and dark can be good
but the humour

I never quite found, that feeling
you'd always be kind of

an object,
for it to be hot.

The bottom was trans
which shouldn't matter

but of course it matters
I needed to watch myself

licking the balls of another
man, laughing

I FEEL LOVE

A needle hits a groove in my brain. 'I Feel Love' comes on, but it isn't love, it's shame, the full extended disco mix that lasts eight minutes then begins again. Another earworm: Are you sorry? Yes. And what are you sorry for? My thoughts, my words, what I have done, what I have failed to do. How seamlessly the songs mash together but nothing nullifies the past, we must simply live with who we are. Shame binds us to each other like a Donna Summer record on a sweaty dancefloor. Every drunk and high vessel, every painful contradiction, deferred in smoke machines and lights, replaced, for a few sweet hours, by something that feels like love.

BLUE ROOM WITH BLUE DILDO

At first you think there's something alive in there,
looking again you realise that sense of movement
comes only from the folds in the room —
the faded stripes of an emerald and off-white
towel, discarded on an unmade duvet. Two duvets,
in case the first fails. Blue autumn light
filters through a translucent blind
and floods the room. The royal blue of the dildo
matches the hemp blanket on the window ledge,
scrunched and lifeless like a person collapsed
after a hit and run. The dildo glistens with lube
upon the towel, remainder of abandoned attempt
at self-sodomy. I'm an optimist —
convinced that dildo will one day fit,
convinced something in that room is still alive.

SHE CAME TO SEE ME LAST NIGHT
BUT LEFT AN HOUR LATER

The 8th Floor!
Thank God I don't want to kill myself.
The view is stunning. A sachet
of instant coffee sustains me.
The sky is bubbling over with grey
clouds like Mordor. I look out
over brown Lego brick buildings
to the docklands where cranes
pierce the black November morning.
My phone tells me weather information
is currently unavailable. (She came to see
me last night but left an hour later.)
My brain tells me to call and tell her it's off
but I know as I peel my shirt off, it's on.
I hand the key card over at reception,
pass through automatic doors, refreshed
after eight hours of nightmares.
And I feel overcome by love for the city
and for the Thames as I cross the bridge
and later that day I will call her and we'll decide
it will definitely be different this time.

IT'S A WONDERFUL LIFE

You want to remember it like a scene from a movie.
Emerging from your friend's tower block at 5am
on Boxing Day to a sky full of snow, wavy on wine
and an unexpected pill, pausing for a moment
before unlocking your bike, dazzled by the brightness.
The roads are empty as you cycle home, the cold
on your face waking every cell of inebriated DNA.
You're horny as hell, mind fixating on how much
you wanted to fuck the postman who'd bought the pills
along, Christmas gifts from someone on his round,
though he himself did not partake. The postman,
a friend of a friend, almost certainly straight.
All you can think of is getting slammed
and how miserable the cold is and all the dumb things
you said. Talking about the agency that turned you down,
saying they had someone else too similar. You said
maybe they had too many white men on their roster
and you meant this in their defence, now you're convinced
it came across bitter and sincere and you sounded like
all the successful white male authors who complain
they are now the marginalised. This is the lasting imprint
of yourself you have probably left forever. That,
and how much you clearly wanted to fuck the postman.
Your leg muscles are tense and achy. The saddle
is against your groin. How needy you are, humping
the bike like a dog. Now you're thinking, even if the postman
had been straight he might have taken a bro-job
or you could have presented your dickless body to him

like it didn't count, like it made you not a man, your dignity
less important than getting railed. Once home you run your tongue
against the indents of your mouth, which is sore from gurning.
You really should sleep, but you end up sharing grubby messages
with terrible men online 'till 7am when your body finally shakes
in a pleasure that immediately regrets itself, regrets the bits of you
you shed across the internet. Nothing's ever deleted now.
Later that day, when you are able to move, you text
a friend to tell them about last night — flakes tumbling down
against the darkness of winter, how you cycled home
through a city asleep but for you and your bike, snow gently
landing on your face, how it was beautiful, like a movie.

X

marks the spot beneath my clavicle
where a lover once took
a thick gauge syringe needle
and watched the red from in me
trickle before we kissed
nothing but blood between us.
Lower, past sparse hairs
and oversized nipples,
two jagged lines of pink
scar tissue, cuts received
willingly. I wanted to feel
icy water against my skin
unrestrained by taut Velcro
and parts unceremoniously tacked on
as seaweed brushed my legs.
I never planned to be marked
but sometimes on an afternoon
I'll wake from the heaviness of dreams
and put a hand to the constellations
of my chest and recall the warmth
of licking the sweat from another
man's armpit on the dancefloor
as his fingers followed my scars.

RETURN TO THE SIXTH FORM COMMON ROOM

A white beam of light is pouring in, particles
of dust form a line, pointing to nothing.
White furniture, white walls, faded navy carpet.
No mocking posters, nothing to remind me this
is the building I learned cruelty earns respect.
Now I see the cheapness of the plastic desks.
No teachers, no absurd rules as I wade through
a sea of empty plastic chairs. Now the threat is gone
I can appreciate there was some peace here. Sixteen
was the first time I got a moment's respite, didn't hear
how low I was in the social order with the same frequency
as the years before. Still, the room must be empty
to be safe, just the beam of light for company.
I still fear the sound of laughter.

TO A LIME

Blood of mojito
Sweet slimy kiss
of amphibian tongue
Shrub of the desert
Sharp as a cadenza
Swift as a slap
Tequila sun-riser
Green as life sliced
open to expose
the moist and pulpy
innards of life
Out of the sandy
nothingness
its light glints
on horizons
like a wish

YOU WILL DREAM ABOUT RABBITS

too many rabbits. You will dream
you are dating a woman from *Mad Men*
who sings you country songs.
You will dream about a sadistic cop
who resembles an actor
who played an ineffectual cop
in a well-known comedy
but there will be nothing funny
about him in your dreams.
You will dream you are a sweet Italian boy
pursued relentlessly by an angry father
who may or may not have killed his mother.
You will be drinking wine with a famous actress
in a cabaret bar in Weimar Berlin when he catches you.
You finally found your place amongst the seedy glamour.
Brutality always finds a way of coming home.

THAT'S NOT A DOG IT'S A

wolf
cloud
devil
sea monster
wiry horse
man in dog costume
hirsute old Major
cluster of impasto brushstrokes
draught excluder
furry pencil
teddy at end of a washing cycle
miniature bear
rug on the lookout
bemused stranger
who wants to sniff you
and eat your arse

SELF-PORTRAIT AS A CROW

I wanted to draw myself as a crow.
Gothic, brooding, coal black
feathers, glinting orbs for eyes.
I read that crows suffered
from existential angst. It excited me
to picture them pecking
at discarded blister packs
of white pills, lying on a bed
of twigs, cawing their dreams
to corvid psychotherapists
who scratch notes in the mud
with their talons, *The patient*
believes he is being watched
by humans. I wanted
to draw a crow as me,
swooping into funerals
dressed as myself, keening
Bauhaus throughout the service.
I heard that crows sometimes had sex
with the dead, I watch them
watching me from a crumbling
place, I can't imagine such an absence
of shame or such artfulness
as to retrieve my condemned
sketches from the bins
at night and build a home.

WE WILL ALL HAVE BED BUGS AND
ANTIBIOTIC-RESISTANT GONORRHOEA

when the drugs stop working
we must learn to see ourselves
as vessels
carrying populations
like dirt
like trees
like streams
like the ink
from old diaries
you try to wash out
in the bath
there comes a time
you must accept
you can't always
tackle the things
inside yourself
by disinfecting
and scrubbing them clean

FORCE MAJEURE

There's a serial killer on the loose and it's definitely one of my friends. Or two. There are usually two just to throw you. This winter I've felt a new sense of inadequacy in my body after a friend surveyed it as you would a disappointing present. We weren't even fucking, they weren't even cis. I went to bed angry, picturing their face. They say you shouldn't go to bed angry, but what can you do? Scream? Too conscious of the neighbours for that. Remember that film, *Force Majeure*, where they're at a ski resort in the Alps and the main character is told by his friend that screaming at the top of your lungs is better than years of therapy? He takes up his friend's suggestion and screams into the snowy void. Apparently that film is about masculinity, I've always thought it's about death. Last week I was sick with the possibility of nuclear war, this week I'm acclimatising.

WHY ARE YOU HERE?

Because I wanted to run as far as I could from the pale suburbs
that made me, the nauseating smell of petrol in the backseat of my
parent's car

Because of what they did, in school, to people like me

Because when I moved away, I took it all with me with me

Because I thought I'd try out polyamory for the first time by
fucking everyone over

Because I thought if I moved again, to an even bigger city, the sheer
grey mass would swallow everything distinct and wrong in me

Because the plan was to be anonymous forever

Because when you're queer you're never anonymous

Because the even bigger city became like a party at 8am when it's
light outside and the drugs are wearing off

Because one night in my tenth address of thirteen years, the WiFi
cut out and the mould was spreading across the ceiling and I hid
from my flatmates, drank a bottle of wine and thought, fuck this,
I'm leaving

Because I thought my failings had to be exorcised before my life
could begin

Because there were people who persisted

Because they knew a wood with a cabin near the freezing sea
where it snowed brightly coloured leaves in autumn

Because they took me there in the backseat of their car

ON BOB'S BED, LEEDS, 2005

To achieve harmony in bad taste is the height of elegance.
— Jean Genet

Three-headed tangle of pale feet and legs,
grimy saturation of afternoon light. Greying
socks, Converse shoes on bed, Argos
child's watch. Retro duvet with its many shades
of green, undoubtedly the most tasteful thing
in that house, even after its absorption
of sweat and cum and blackcurrant-tinged
cider, prelapsarian after every wash.
Lover on one side, friend on the other,
it doesn't matter who was who, people
were always merging. The lover and me
always breaking up, becoming friends,
falling into bed again, therapists asking,
why don't you just cut contact, as if young
queers in a small city can avoid each other,
as if we'd want to. The friend and me
would spoon in a single bed, once leading
to a transmission of scabies. Who took the photo?
We look too at ease for an audience
but I'm avoiding eye-contact with someone.
Hiding my face beneath a freshly dyed 90s
boyband fringe, lest the camera expose too much of it.
Clutching orange mugs from the German market,
exchanged for a deposit, used as wine glasses.
Two bottles for a fiver from the shop on the corner
we visited each night. Her hair and mine merge
into one animal, his long arm relaxes around us both.

Two of us were in a band, when we played we wore
electrical tape over our four nipples, blade runner make-up
and very little else. 'This is like our version of having sex,'
my bandmate said as we planned to urinate
on each other for an outdoor performance.
Practiced in the bath, losing it in a fit of giggles
at the golden streams, feeling like kids again.
I lost my nerve when it came to the show,
but we were already part of each other.

PANDAS
After Jane Yeh

No
We don't want to
All we want to do
is sit
chew bamboo
roll over
each other
not like that
but most of all
sleep
Why the pressure
to reproduce
when the planet
is dying anyway?
You tank the
whole thing
and expect us
to put our cubs
on the fire
Don't humour us
Don't dress up
in those tacky
fake fur suits
and pretend to be us
We aren't stupid
We can recognise
the smell
of your kind

a mile off

wreaking of

apocalyptic charity

We exist

It's never enough for you

ANTICHRIST

I don't remember
where we'd been
but when we got back
we watched *Antichrist*,
a film we'd talked about so long,
I'd never had the guts to watch.
That scene came on, I looked away,
but she was strict and played it
twice, saying I'd regret the lack
of closure. She knew me, she was right.
Was it the scissors, the deer, the fox,
whatever the fuck was going on,
the mumblings in black and white
that starred up one of many blurry
2ams or that as we watched
we saw the funny side?
Shit, mate, well if you don't laugh
you cry. In the darkness
of her flat we too were watched,
chugging our pre-mixed
alcoholic tins, by posters
of Bikini Kill, a young man
sucking his own cock, silk screen
prints of Derek Jarman's garden,
secateurs for her
unchaotic plants.

THE FRUIT FLIES

Huge eyes and tiny bodies.
They are not smart but they
will outlive us all. Oblivious
as I play the violin. Oblivious
to the music of the radio
in the morning.
Nothing phases them. Nothing
puts them off as they gorge
on the sweetness of wine
or plums or whatever mess
remains. Nothing stops
their relentless breeding,
joyful orgies, multiplying
bodies do not know how
unwelcome they are.
Every time I turn the light on
there are more, on every mottled
surface, divine state of just living,
fucking, dying. No existential angst,
no nuclear war, isn't that
the mindfulness we're all striving for?
I can't see each body as a separate entity,
maybe that's wrong, but to me
they share a brain, is that intimacy?
All they do is as programmed
but I'm the same, reaching
for the sweet nectar
of a bottle, again and again.

0 BPM

It's enough to be alive
even when your heart
has stopped
and you're buried
beneath the surface
of a frozen lake,
no longer sure
where the ice ends
and you begin.
Somewhere
in the flattened waves
of your brain it's enough
to know one morning
the ice will turn to water
and you'll wake
from your trance
to the silent beat
before the dance
resumes and the living
must again be faced.

STEALTH

Sinking naked into the bath
it's easy to forget your body
is a war. If you stay away
from dismembered voices
that want to dig up your skeleton,
measure your skull and tell
you who you are, your life
can be peaceful. You become
a barnacled wreck, only found
by jumping from the ocean's ledge,
descending the Mariana Trench,
where your most contentious
organs turn to paste beneath
the weight of water
and undiscovered fish glide through
your bones without comment.
Somewhere in the wreck is a black box
recording of a night in Wolverhampton
when you were decked out
in eyeliner and leopard print
from New Look, teenage imitation
of Brian Molko. A child asked
if you could spare some change
and when you said no, grabbed
your chest for a humiliatingly
long time. Your friend laughed.
You laughed. What else can be done
when you're assaulted by a ten year old?

And how do you recall this?
And how do you speak of such
things without giving too much
to your enemies? The Black Box sinks
into the silt of history and is lost
like the cemeteries you'd soon
be sneaking into, fellating
men before their fingers sank into
your jeans and made their discovery.
Lost like the water of every bath
that knew your body intimately and held it
with an acceptance you've yet to feel.

DAVID LYNCH IN GLASGOW

Stepping out of the cinema onto wet tarmac, I am flanked by quiet tenements and glowing fog.

A seedy low-rise hotel on Argyll Street looks invitingly warm against the night.

The few lights illuminate perspiration-drenched windows, shapes of figures in the steam.

Beyond the hotel, the Clyde is black, no one around but the uniformity of trees at equidistant intervals in beds of white concrete, like rows of cactus plants in a suburban LA home.

Through the corrugated iron industrial estate, Nicholas Cage sings absurdly in my ears.

A brown envelope containing a VHS tape greets me at my doorstep, I swear I will never watch it, but one day I will.

SEA TURTLES

They hatch on empty beaches,
emerging under moonlight, like a cult.
Out pokes a head, pushing grains
of sand apart, then a flipper, smaller
than a human finger. Those not lost
to light pollution will make their way
towards the ocean, across the beach
in unison, trusting it will hold them.
The seas join up eventually
become an inadequacy of water
that fails rusty fishing trawlers
crammed with the desperate.
When waves cross out the sky
and vultures wait on every shore
what else is there to do but trust?

ISOLATION

When I got out of isolation
beneath the February sun
I saw a robin and a great tit
trilling on the pulsing
branches of a naked tree

A private recital
the birds unbothered
by my presence
carried on
as I got closer

I was so accustomed
to those plump bodies
flying from me
in panic
I didn't know
what to do

Eventually
I did as anyone would
and took the phone
from my pocket
so everyone
would know

As I withdrew the thing
the birds flew
from me
landing on branches
out of shot
I stood bewildered
and put the thing away

The robin returned
to its first place
I watched
the inside of its mouth
tongue moving
as it sang
rise and fall of its warm red throat
I remember it as red
I could not look away

I saw how it would
feel to touch the
feathered bulge
and something
in me withers
without touch
that's why we take pictures
though it ruins everything
that one day
we might be touched again

THE TOWER

It took a single bolt of lightning to smash
the shoddy workmanship of my facade.
Took being cast out, exposed
to the cold glow of madness, going
somewhere I might never return,
still it waits like a hospital ward.
That's how closeness feels —
when you're stripped, flogged within
a dungeon. I never rule out the possibility
of anything, like today being better
or my foundations crumbling, or the morning
sun after the defenestration of the hopes
of the day before, falling back
in through the window, painting another
in gold over the beige, anaemic walls.

I LUV THE VALLEY OH!

A pill, not sugar but snow, full of arctic circles, slowly makes its way down the oesophageal tract, freezing each crimson-brown channel as it passes. It's January 2011 and the boiler has been out for months. We huddle in the darkness on the sofa, drinking red wine, watching *True Blood*, opening the slumlord's mail, our attempt at revenge. At night I sleep in my hoodie, hugging the pillow or whoever's rapidly cooling body is available, wishing they were someone else. I'm trying to stay off medication, sometimes I scream into the pillow, never producing the right howl, the kind that reverberates through the body, shakes snow from trees, echoes through a silent valley. If I could scream like that, things would be different, I'm sure. One night, as we sit in front of the TV watching our breath, a shivering housemate enters clutching a half-drunk bottle of Kraken rum and looks at me like I'm a ghost. She tells me she just saw me go upstairs. I haven't moved all evening. No explanation is ever found. Sometimes we talk about Other Len, Bad Len, a malevolent spirit from a parallel universe, or maybe my soul left my body in search of somewhere warm, like when an ice pill melts and memories thaw in the light.

EXIT POP-UP
after Edwin Morgan

Before you go,
if you go, wait —
just one moment of your time.
If you're not here
I'm not here
remembering your face
warmly lit as if
by candles in a church.
The light was blue
and showed you at your best
while in the night outside it rained.
Though every lousy scientist
tells me you'll be back
if you should really want to go
and I should want to die,
one small favour,
trust me, know this—
I'll never share the things you shared
the sequestered parts of you, unless—

THE HOUSE BLEW UP

The family act
like it's a normal evening.

I'm flapping
clammy hands, too aware

of the ticking
in the basement. Dad says:

We cannot just evacuate like hysterics.
We must do things properly.

The dining room is laid out
for the sake of the table,

the people an afterthought,
squeezed between wood and wall,

not enough space to get out
quickly when the time comes.

Dad cooks. He's the only
one who can be trusted.

Well, says mum, setting down food,
last meal before . . . Duh-duh duh duh duuuh!

She gives a hint of jazz hands, puts on
a dramatic voice, as if the impending explosion

were an amateur play starring one of us.
As usual, dad and Jack, who has just discovered

communism, argue about politics.
As usual, I remain silent.

Half an hour to go, mum says,
and we haven't even done the dishes.

Why are you sulking? Dad demands.
You always say that when you're sulking.

The clock ticks.
What is it now?

I know I'm wrong
to be scared. One minute.

Mum is still doing the dishes,
singing to herself.

What have you got to say?
He knows my mouth won't open.

I hold in a scream.
One second. *Well?*

AT DUSK

I walk to the flag pole, the city twinkling
below me. I never noticed till today
you can see the university among the distant
crawl of tiny glowing cars and chalky smears
of cloud above black hills enclosing the city.
Back on street level I pass a mosque, melodic
incantations coming from inside, lights of shops
and tenements, hopeful dogs, huddles of men
smoking, dead patches of silence and dark.
A group of kids, one shouting, 'I love this time
of year, bro!' It's autumn, the air smells of it.
At home, I finally respond to a message from someone
who happens to share my name. 'Len, I'm so sorry
I took so long to get back to you.'

NOTES

Bodily Fluids contains a line from the poem 'Half-Light' by Frank Bidart

Ode to Vega — After the character Vega in the computer game *Street Fighter II*. 'Did my beauty intoxicate you?' was a taunt used by Vega after winning a match.

I make people into my dad is made up of quotations from *The Sluts* by Dennis Cooper

I Feel Love — Takes its title from the song by Donna Summer

It's a Wonderful Life — Takes its title from the 1946 Frank Capra film

Force Majeure — Takes its title from the 2014 Ruben Östlund film

Pandas — After 'An American Panda Leaves the National Zoo' by Jane Yeh

Antichrist — Takes its title from the 2009 Lars von Trier film

The Tower — After the major arcana tarot card

I Luv the Valley OH! — Takes its title from the song by Xiu Xiu

Exit Pop-Up — After 'When You Go' by Edwin Morgan

ACKNOWLEDGEMENTS

Poems from this collection have previously appeared in the following publications: *Impossible Archetype, The North, Anthropocene, Fourteen Poems, Magma, Strings, Spaces of Significance* (Off the Chest, 2024), *Bi+ Lines* (Fourteen Poems, 2023), *Almanac Journal of Trans Poetics, Untitled: Voices*. I am grateful to all the editors for including me. Thank you to Aaron Kent and Broken Sleep Books for publishing this collection.

Bodily Fluids was greatly improved thanks to the thoughtful and generous feedback of Andrew McMillan. I also want to thank Swithun Cooper and Nadine El-Enany for their feedback and encouragement. Thanks Bob Henderson for the source material, Keenan Lew and Faryal Velmi for the creative kinship. Thanks to JJ Brazil, Robin Duval, Madeleine Hunter, Melissa Rakshana Steiner, Lindsay Tudor-Kasbohm and all my friends in Glasgow, London, Leeds and beyond. Thanks Creative Scotland for the financial support. Thank you Cody for making me a better human.

LAY OUT YOUR UNREST

www.ingramcontent.com/pod-product-compliance
Lightning Source LLC
Chambersburg PA
CBHW020218090426
42734CB00008B/1116